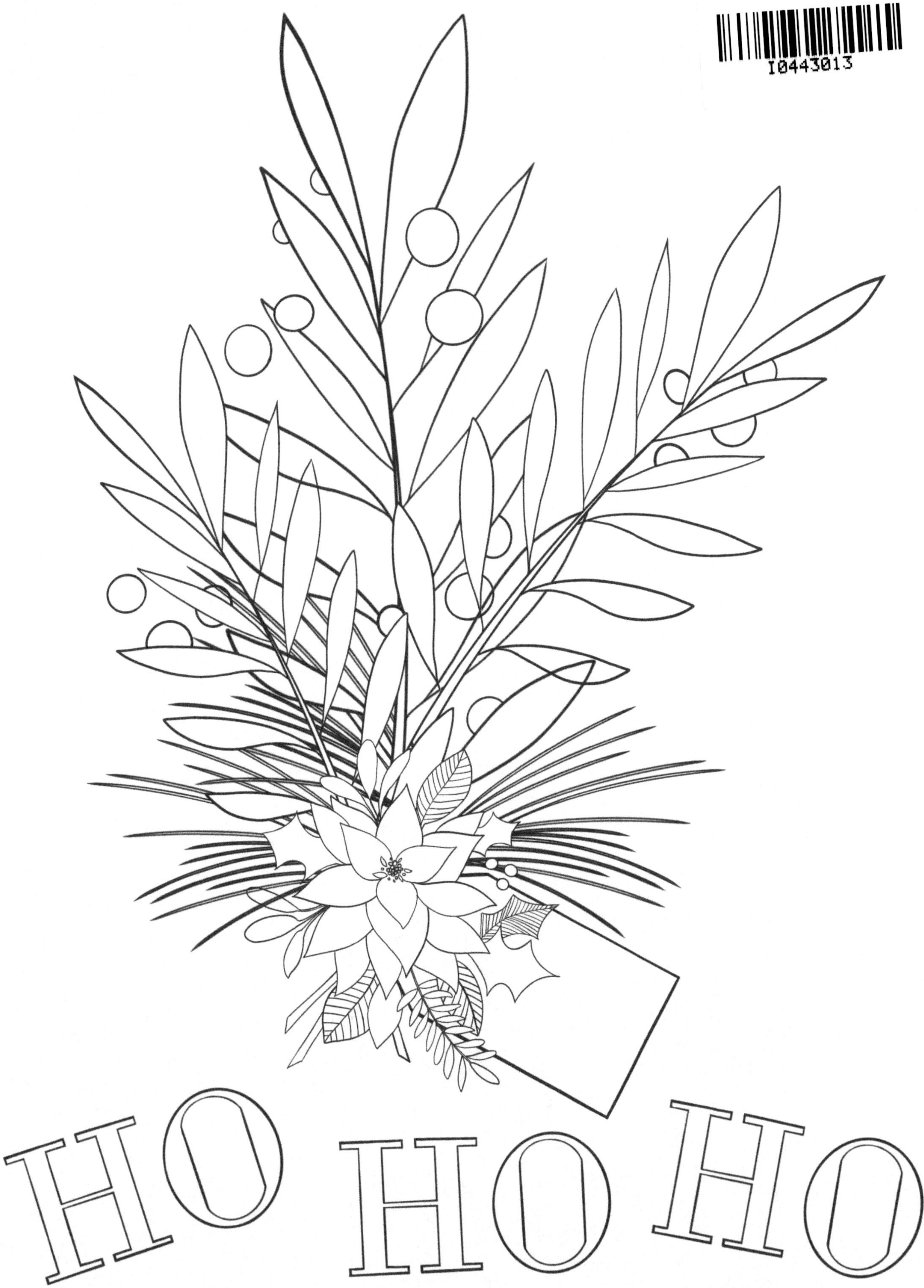
HO HO HO

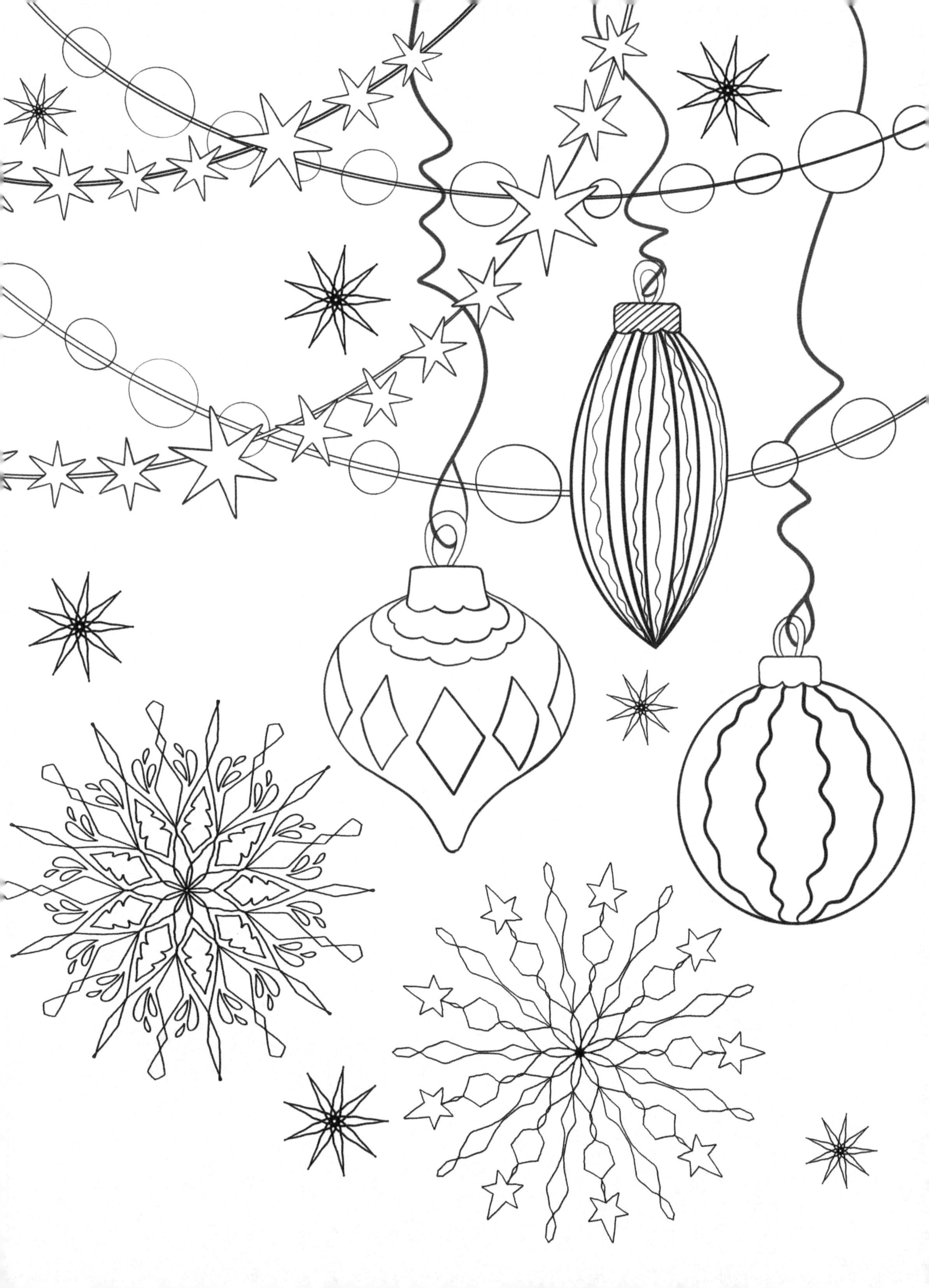

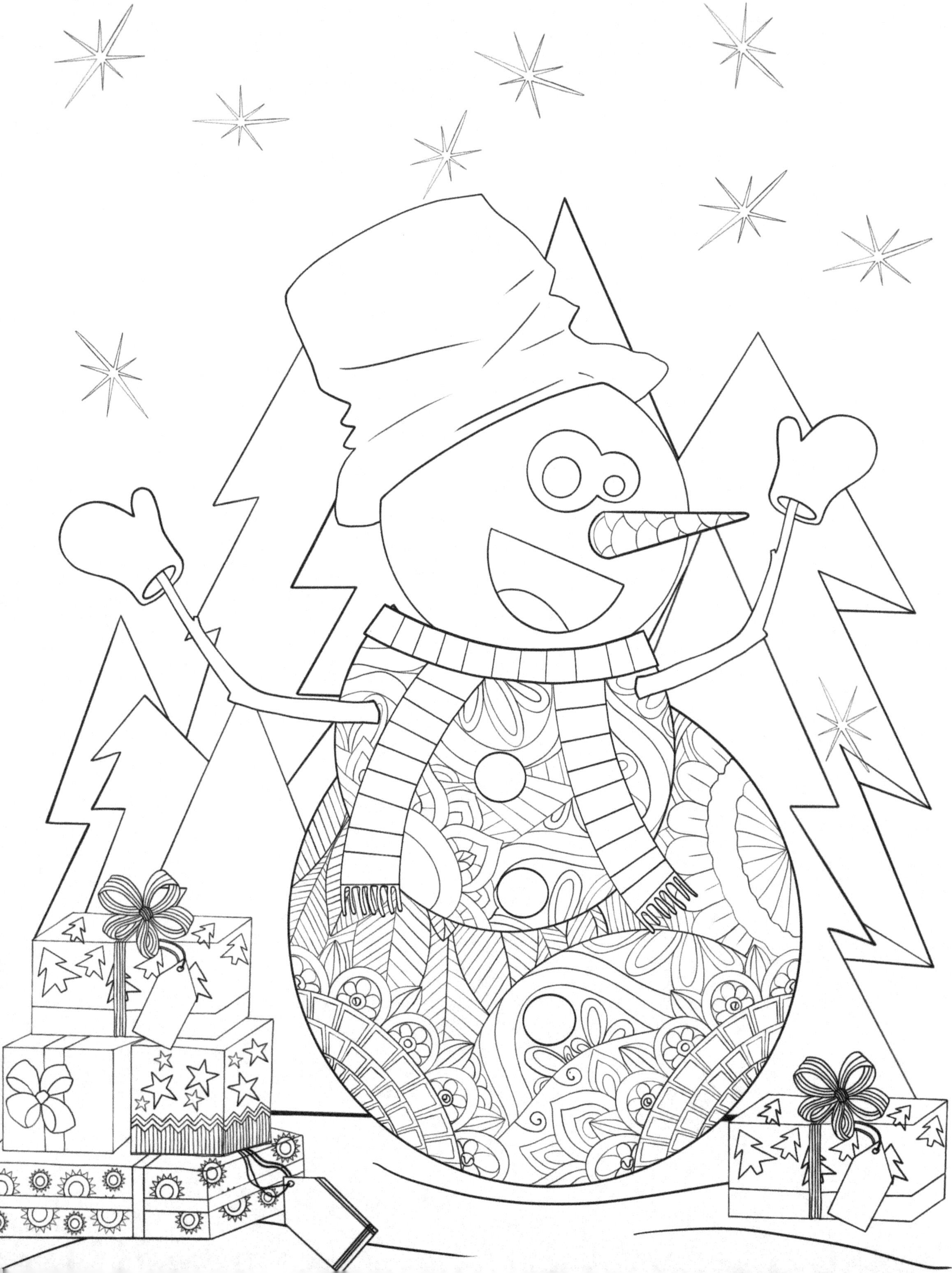

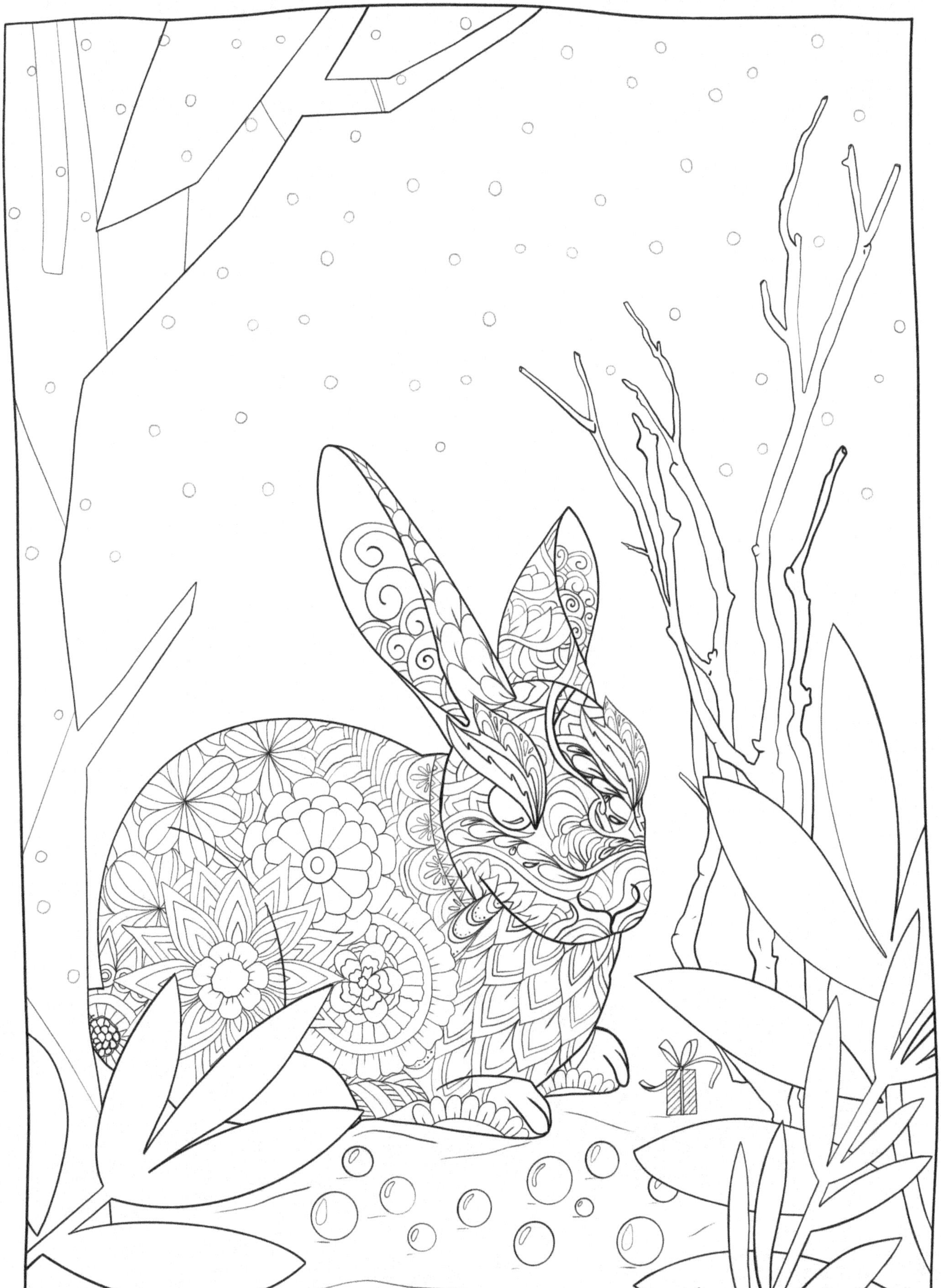

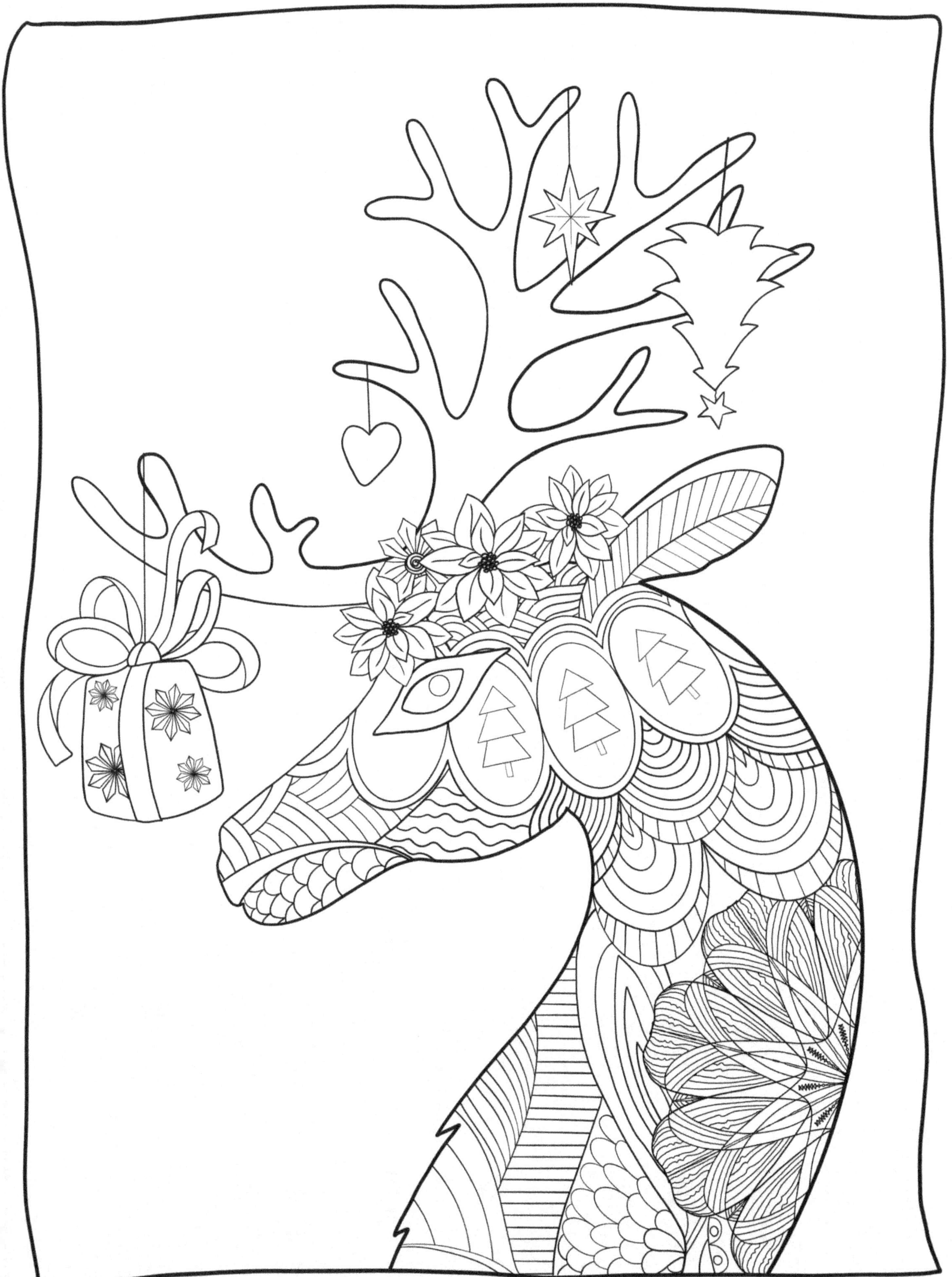

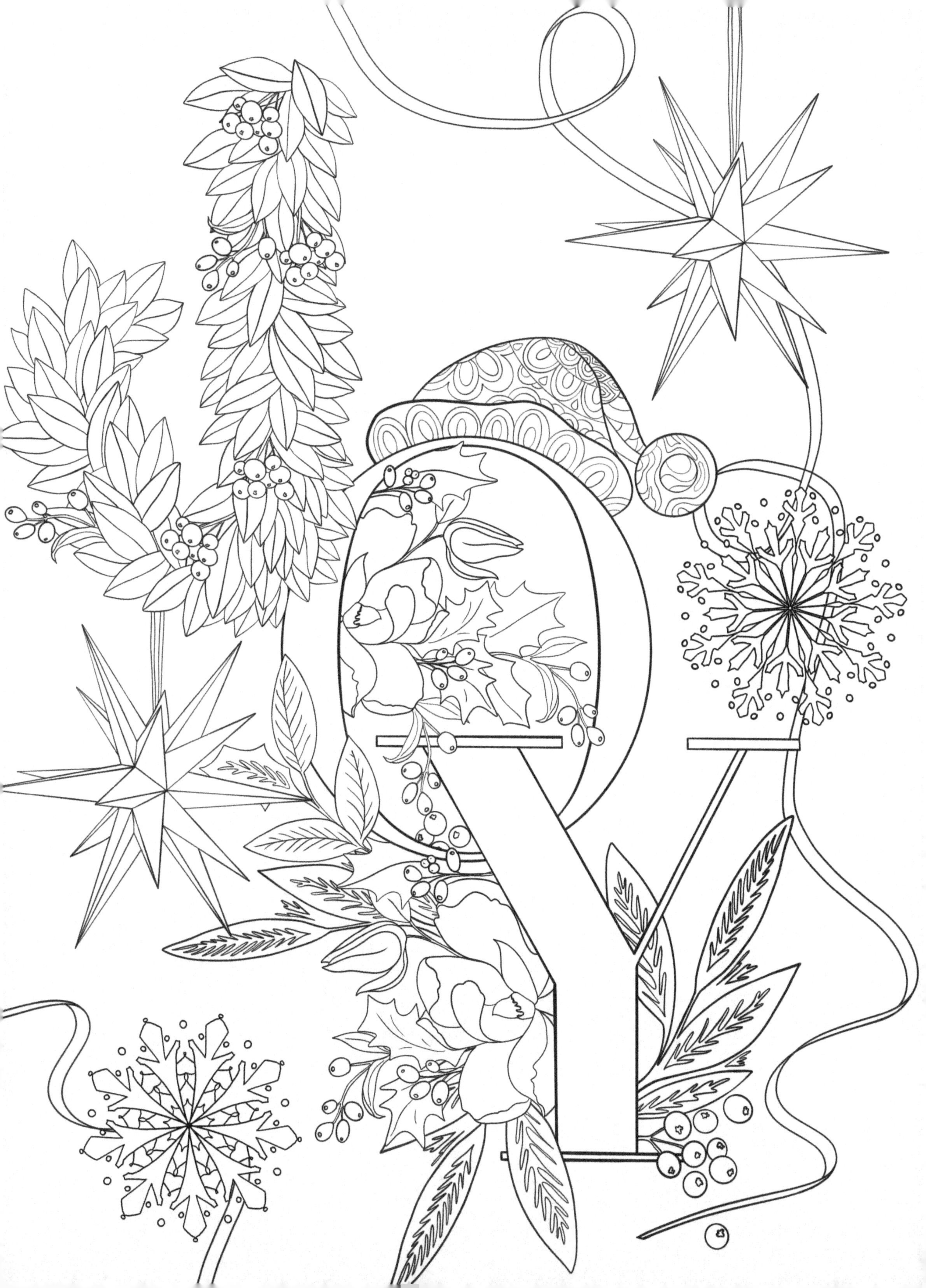
OY

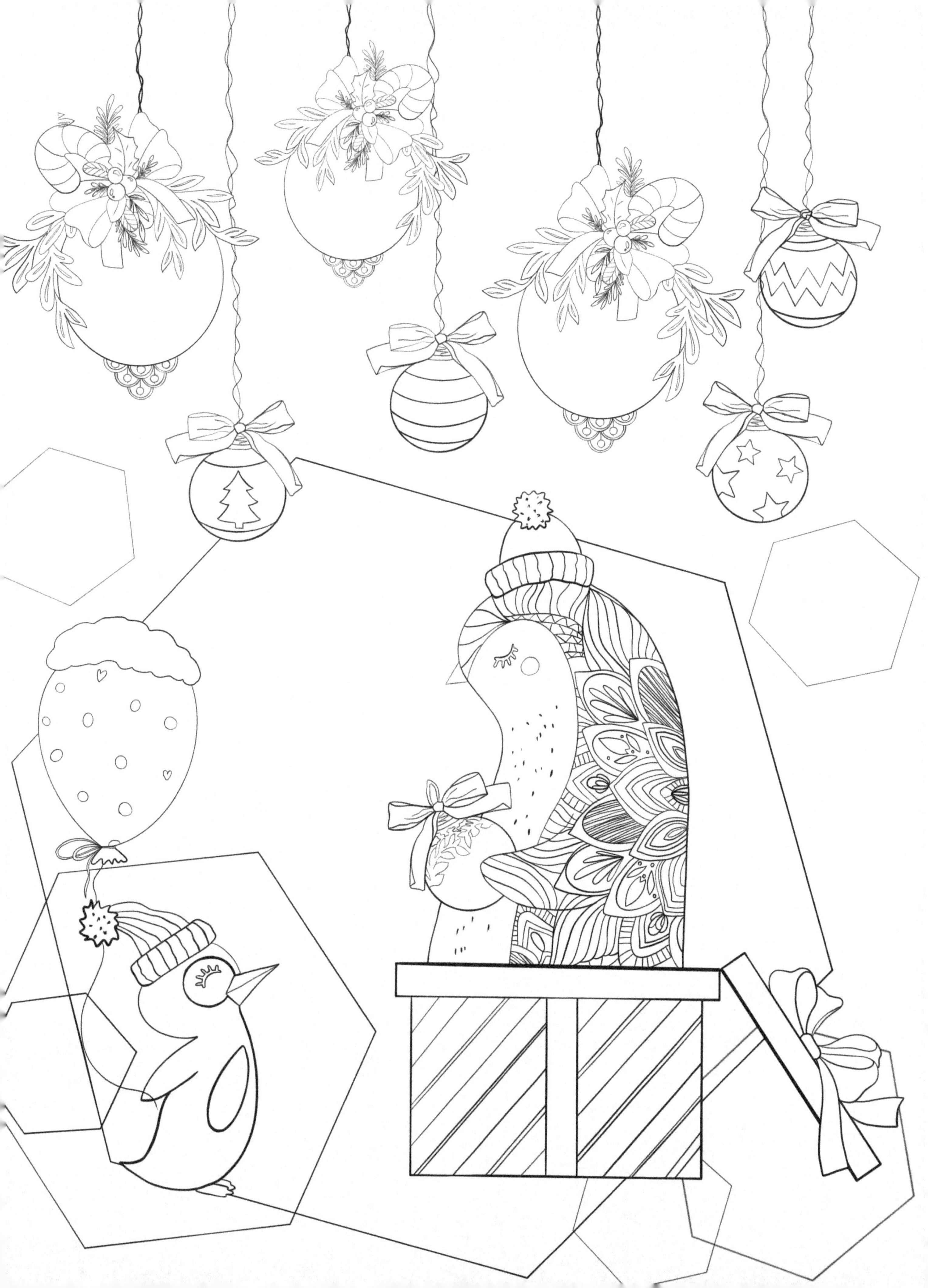

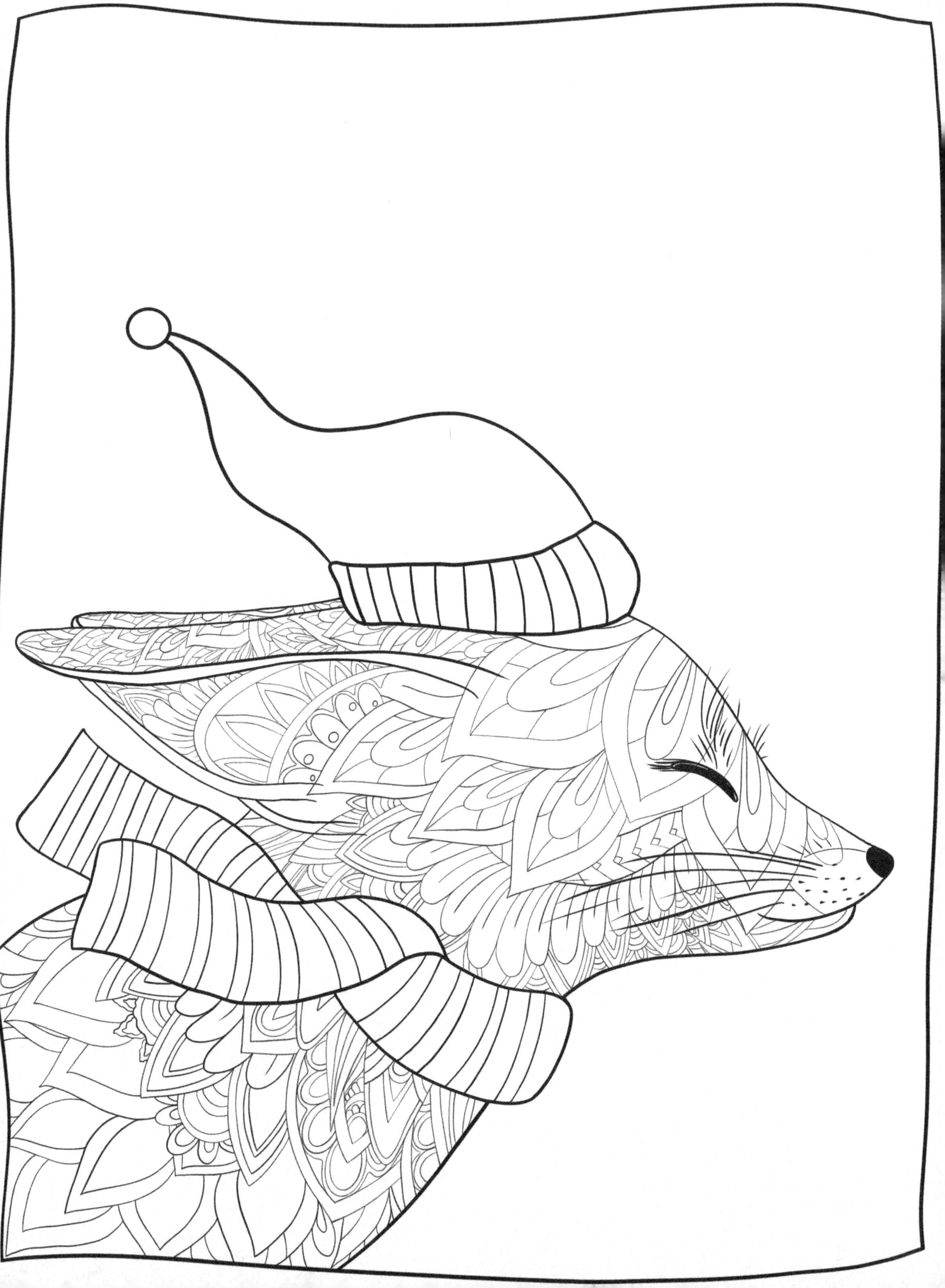

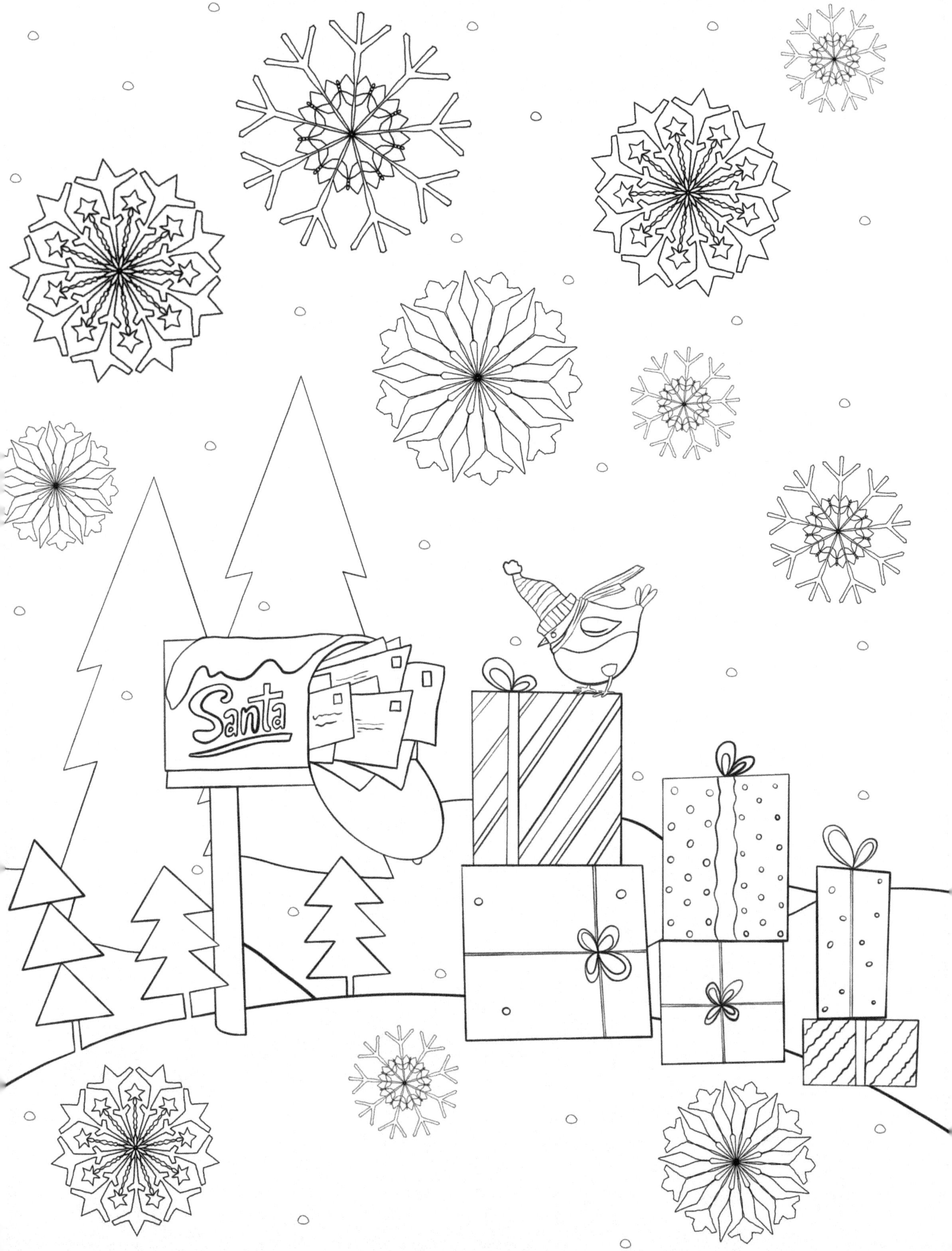
Santa

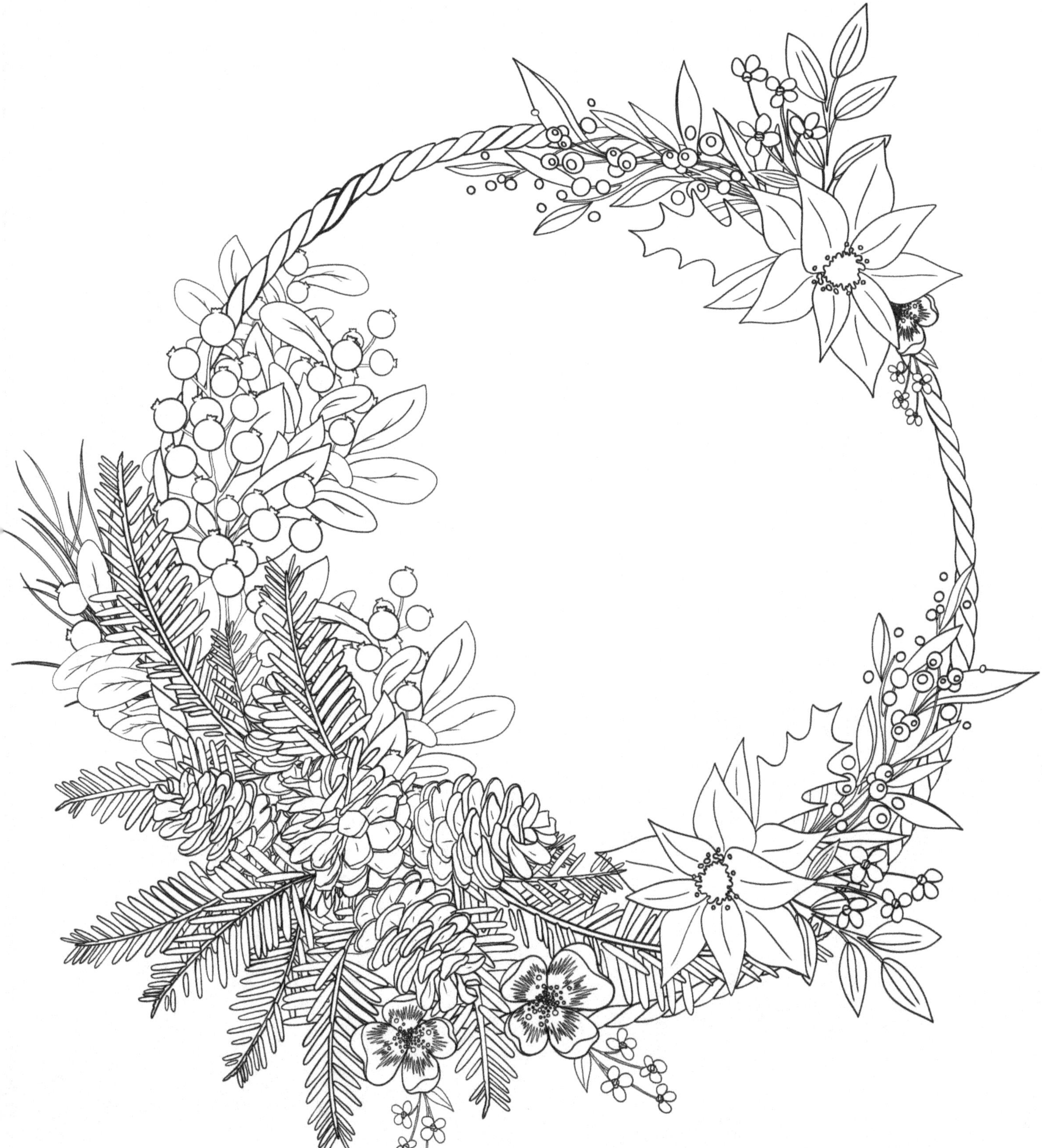

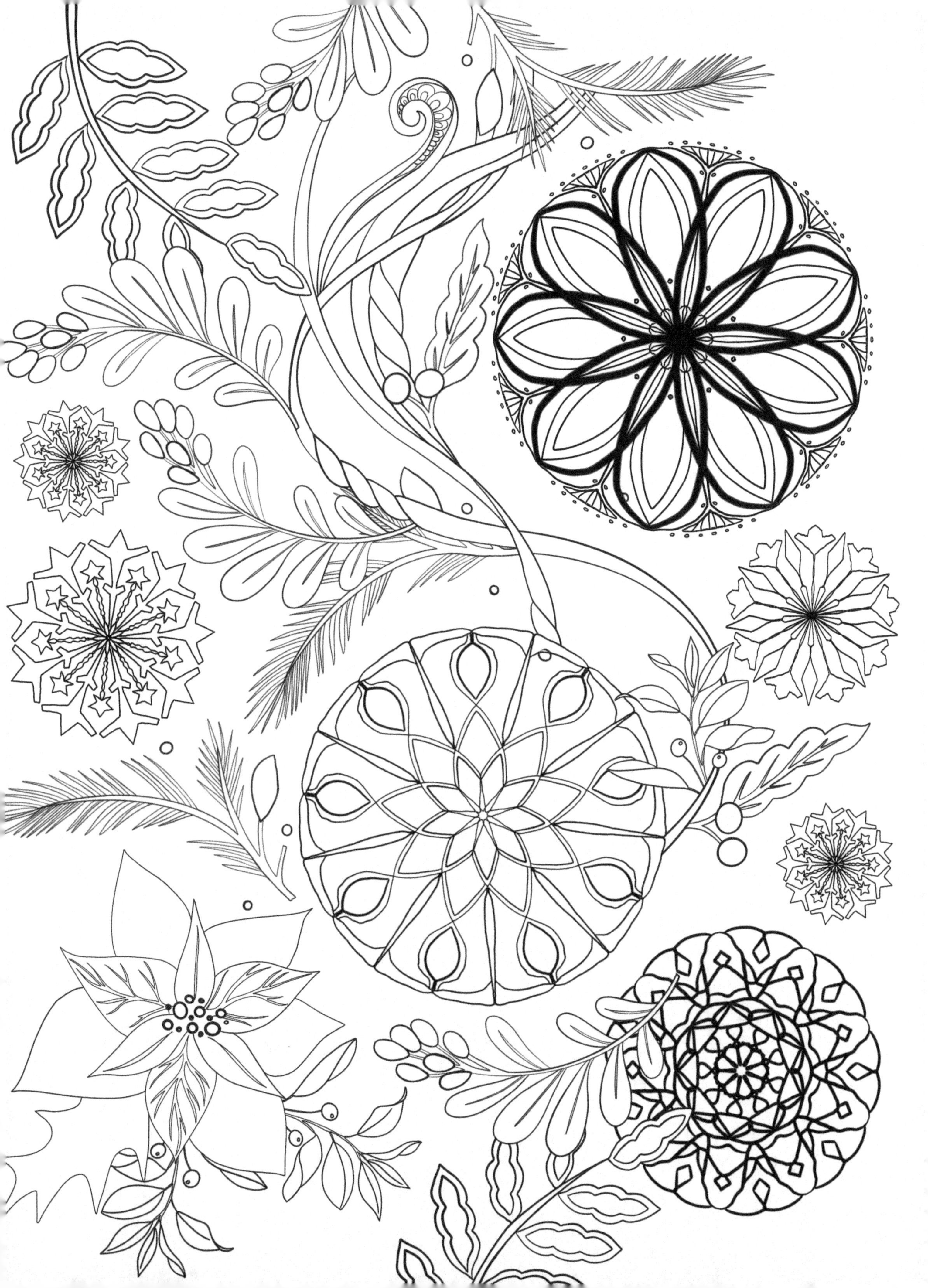

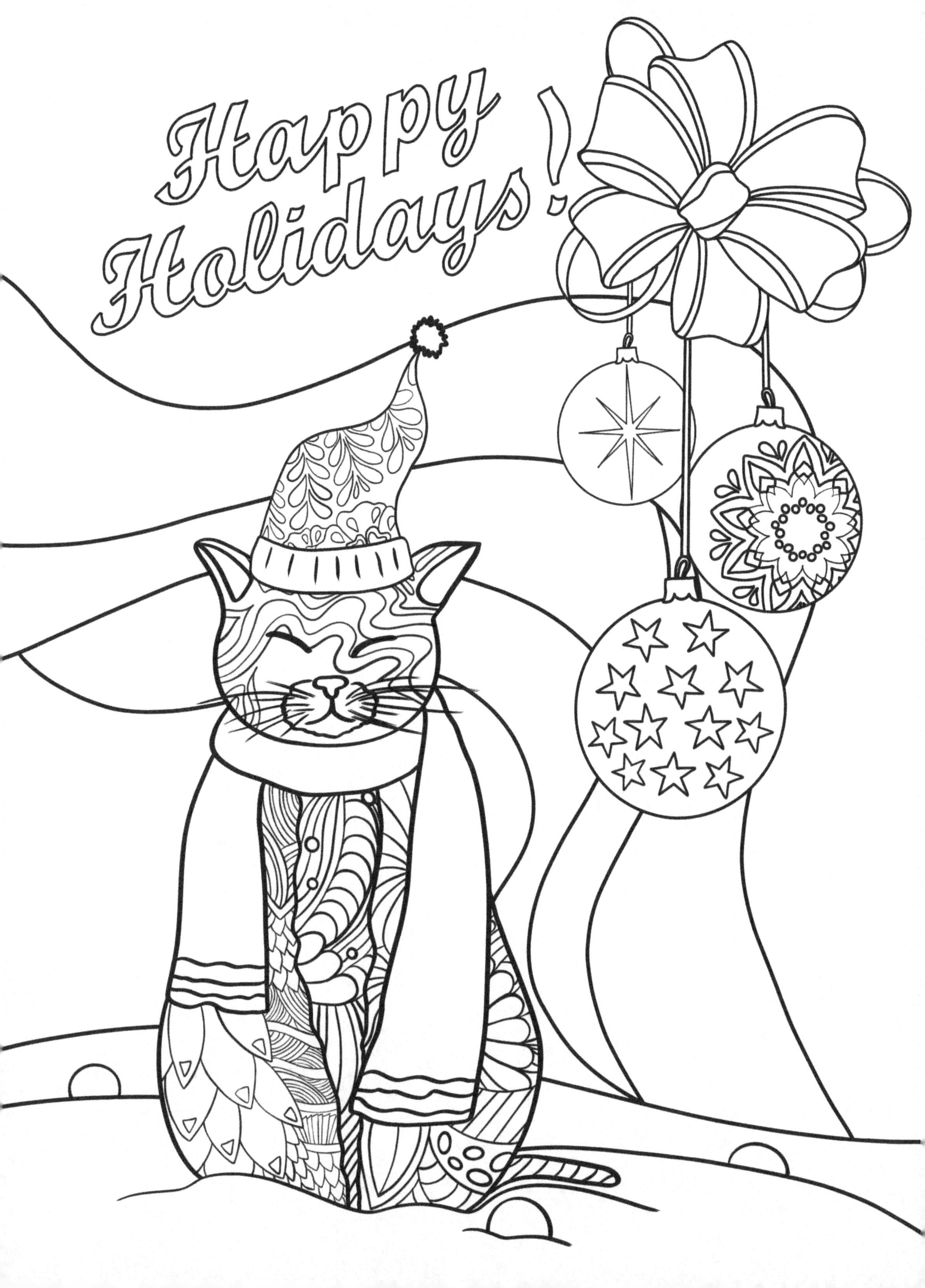
Happy Holidays!

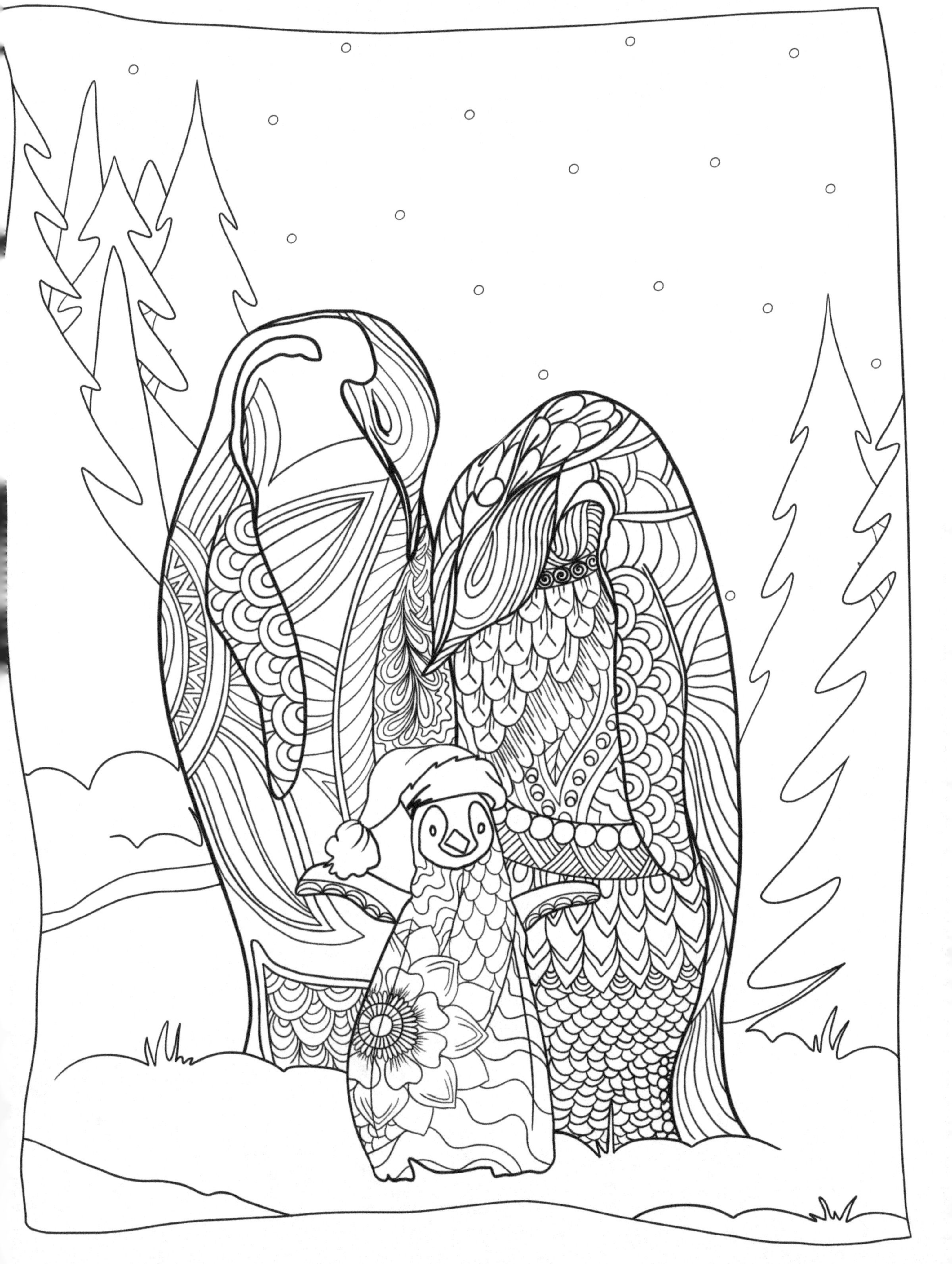

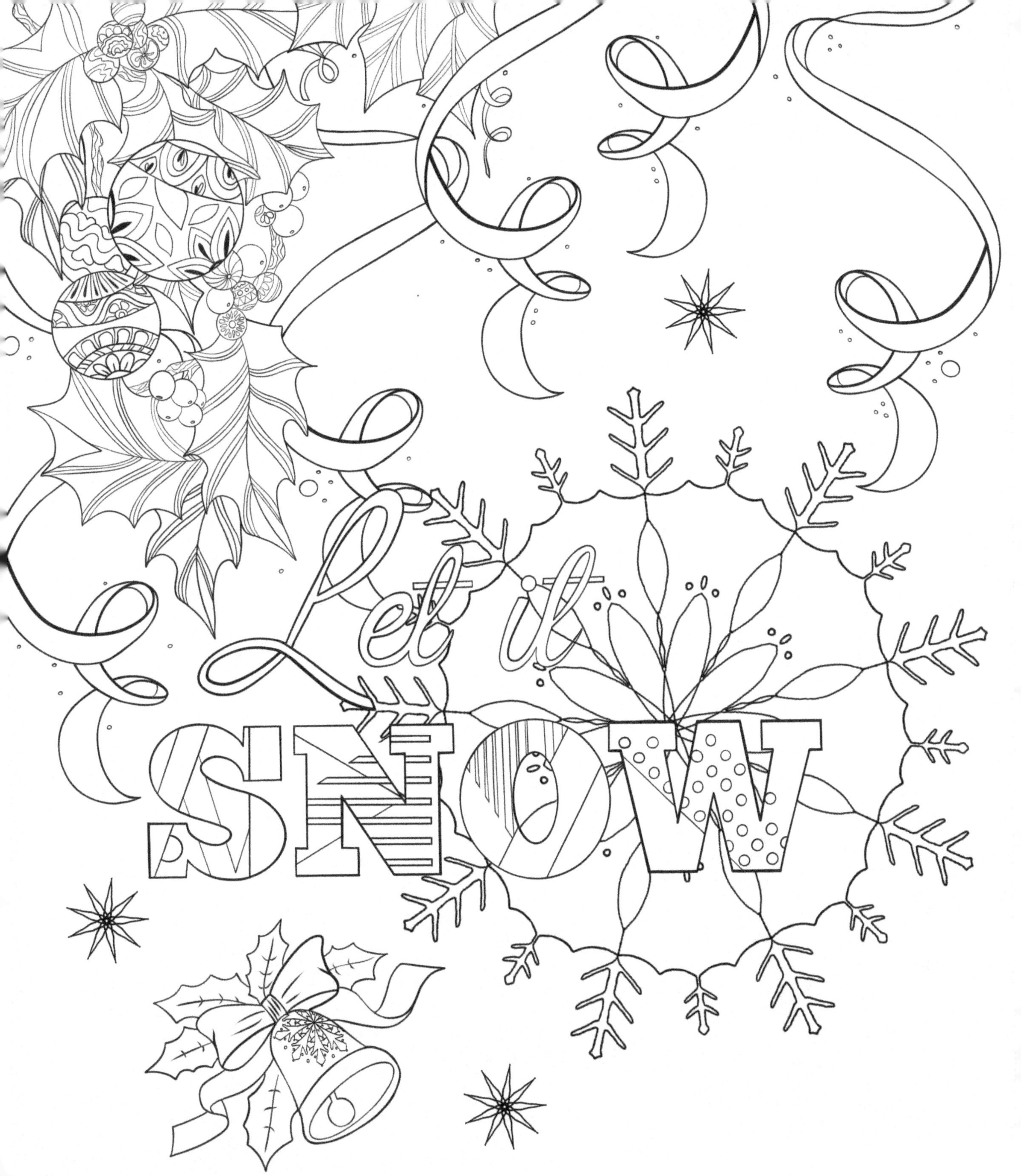
Let it
SNOW

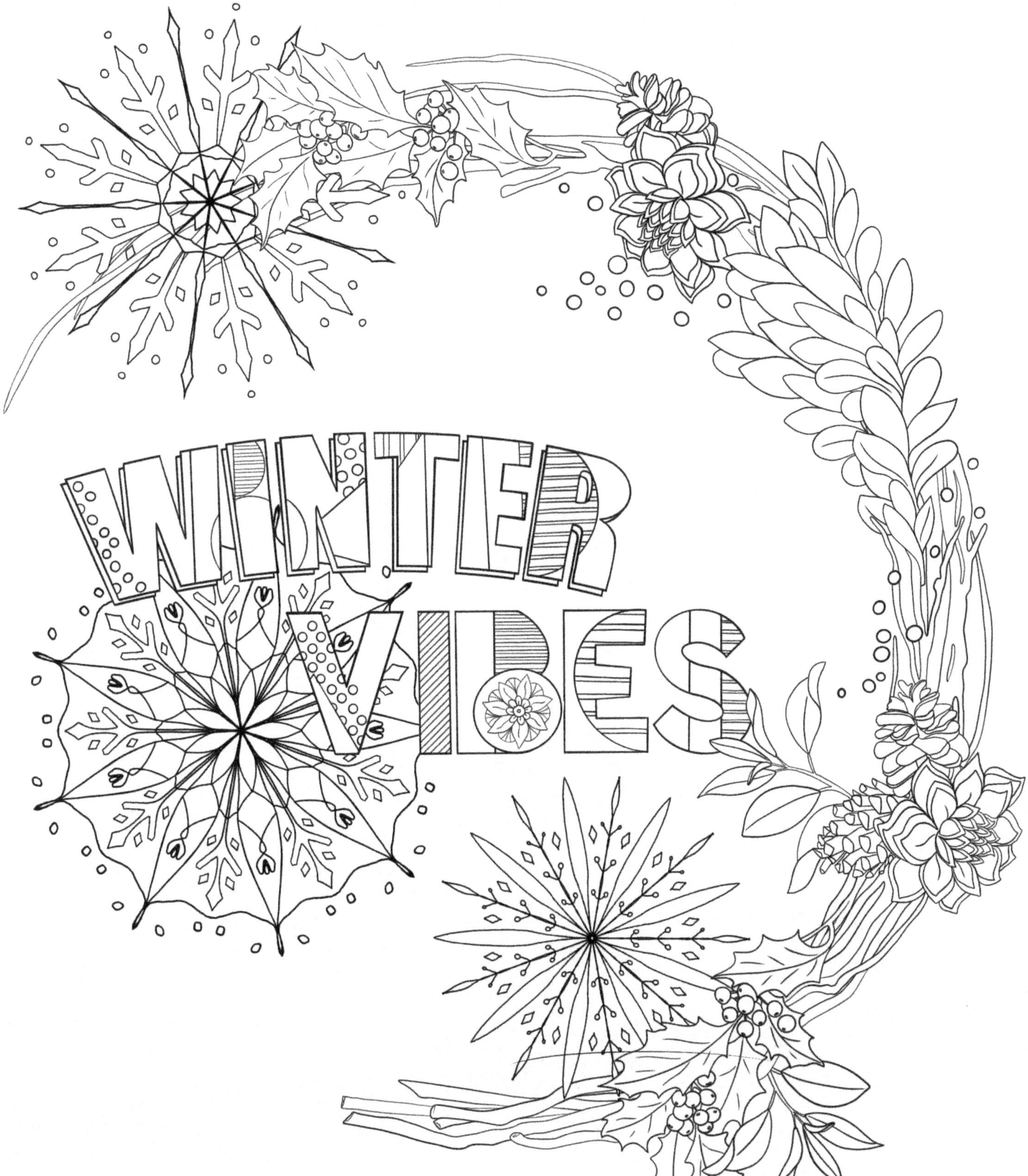
WINTER
VIBES

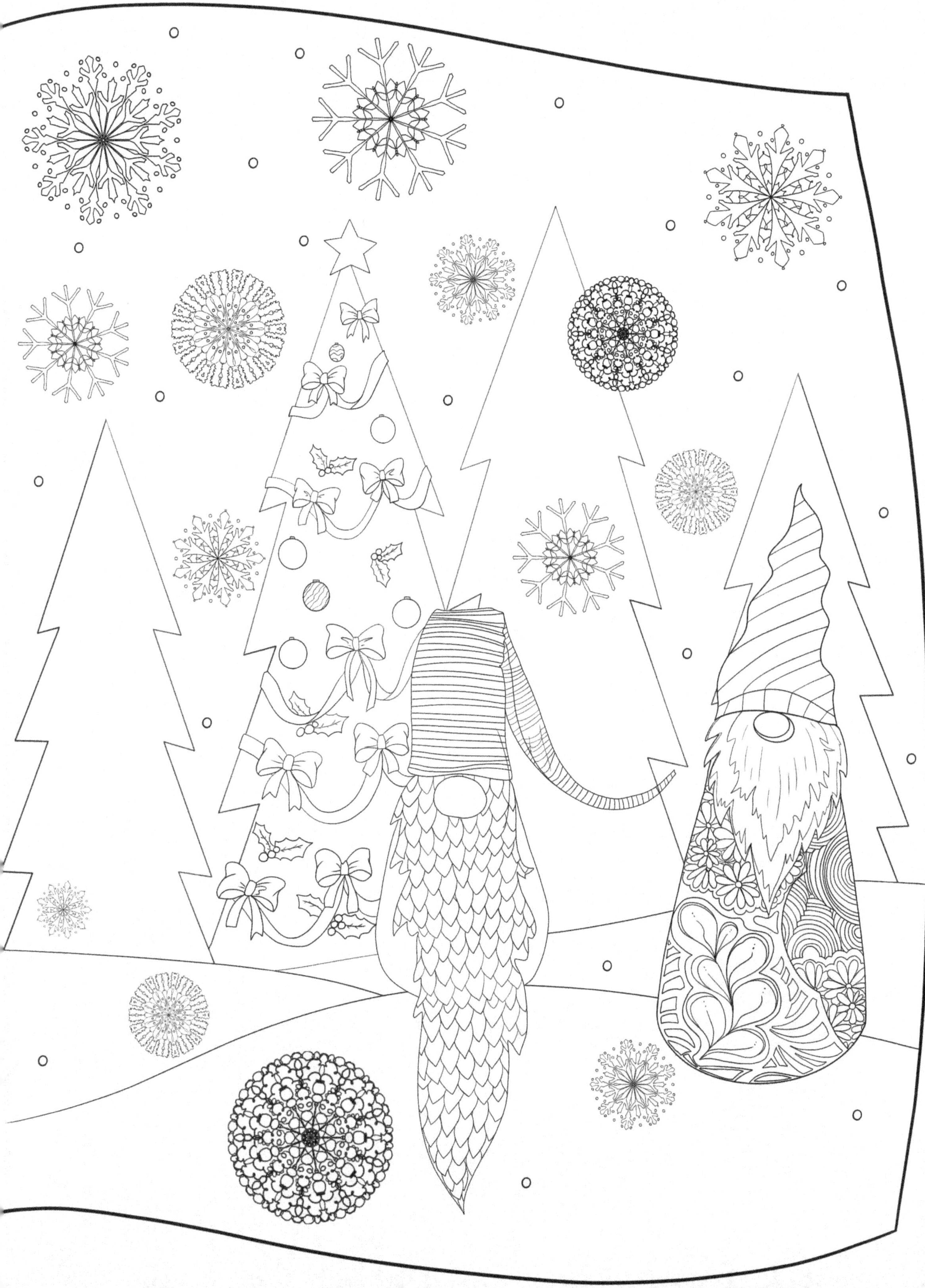

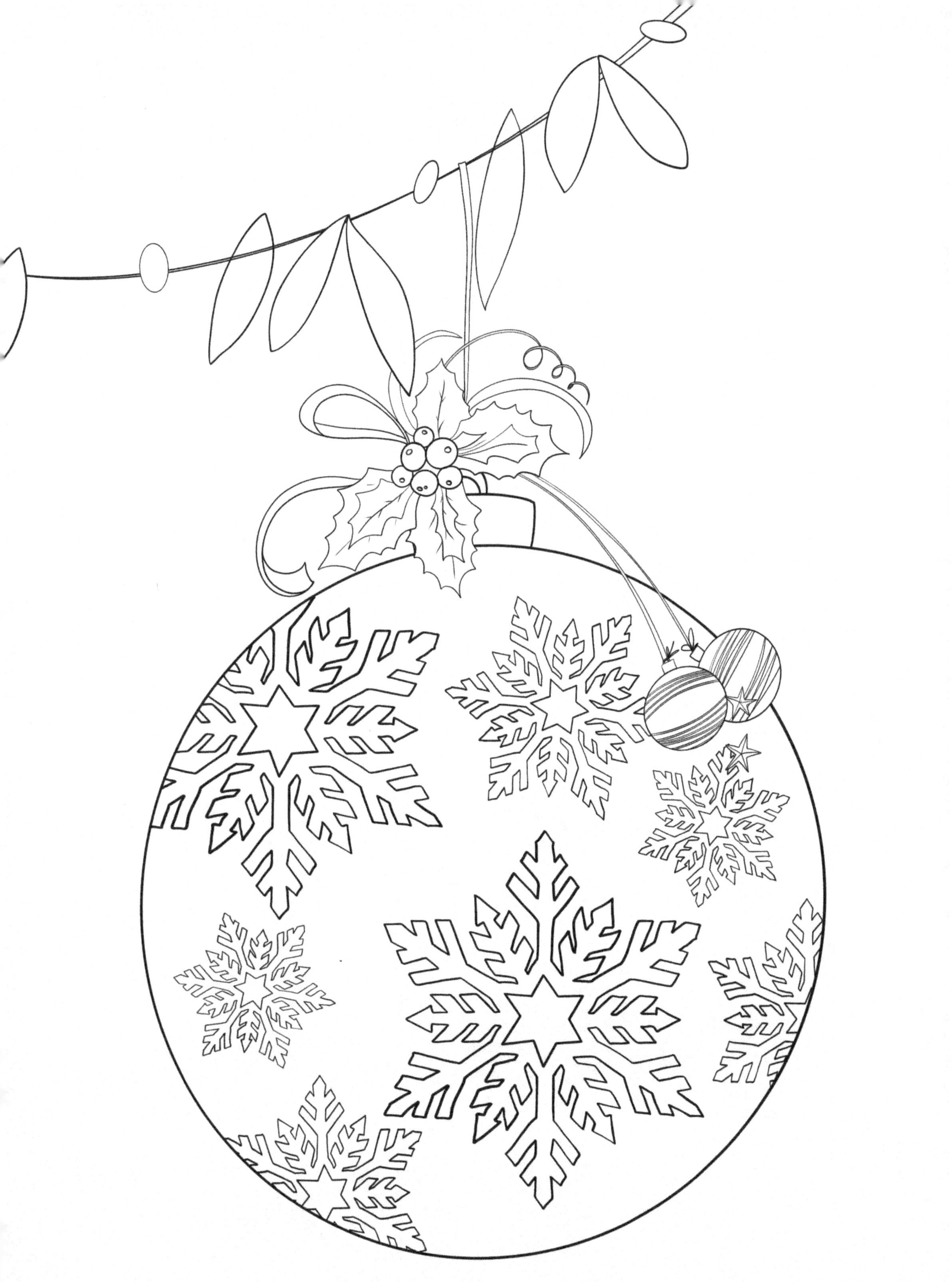

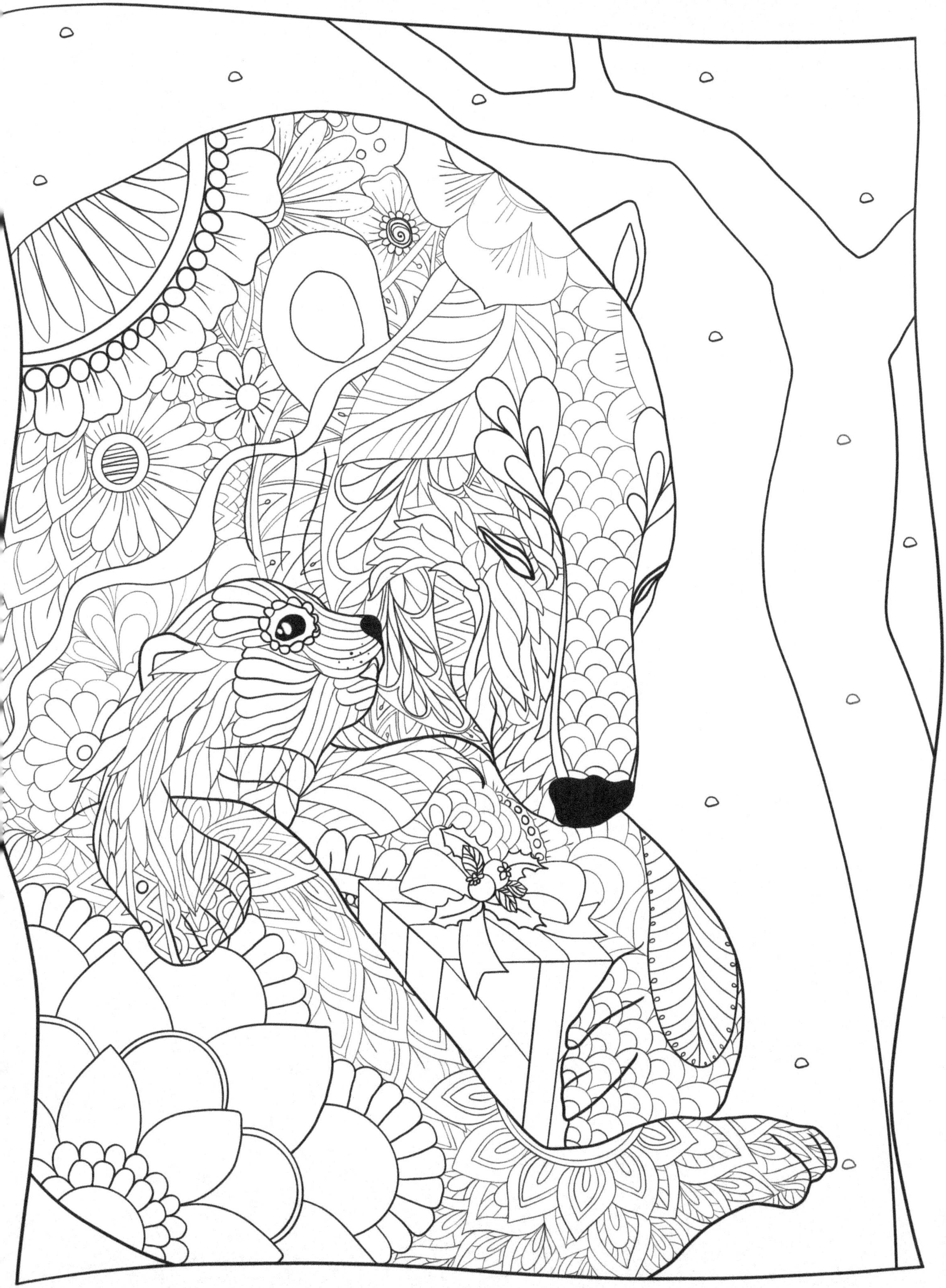

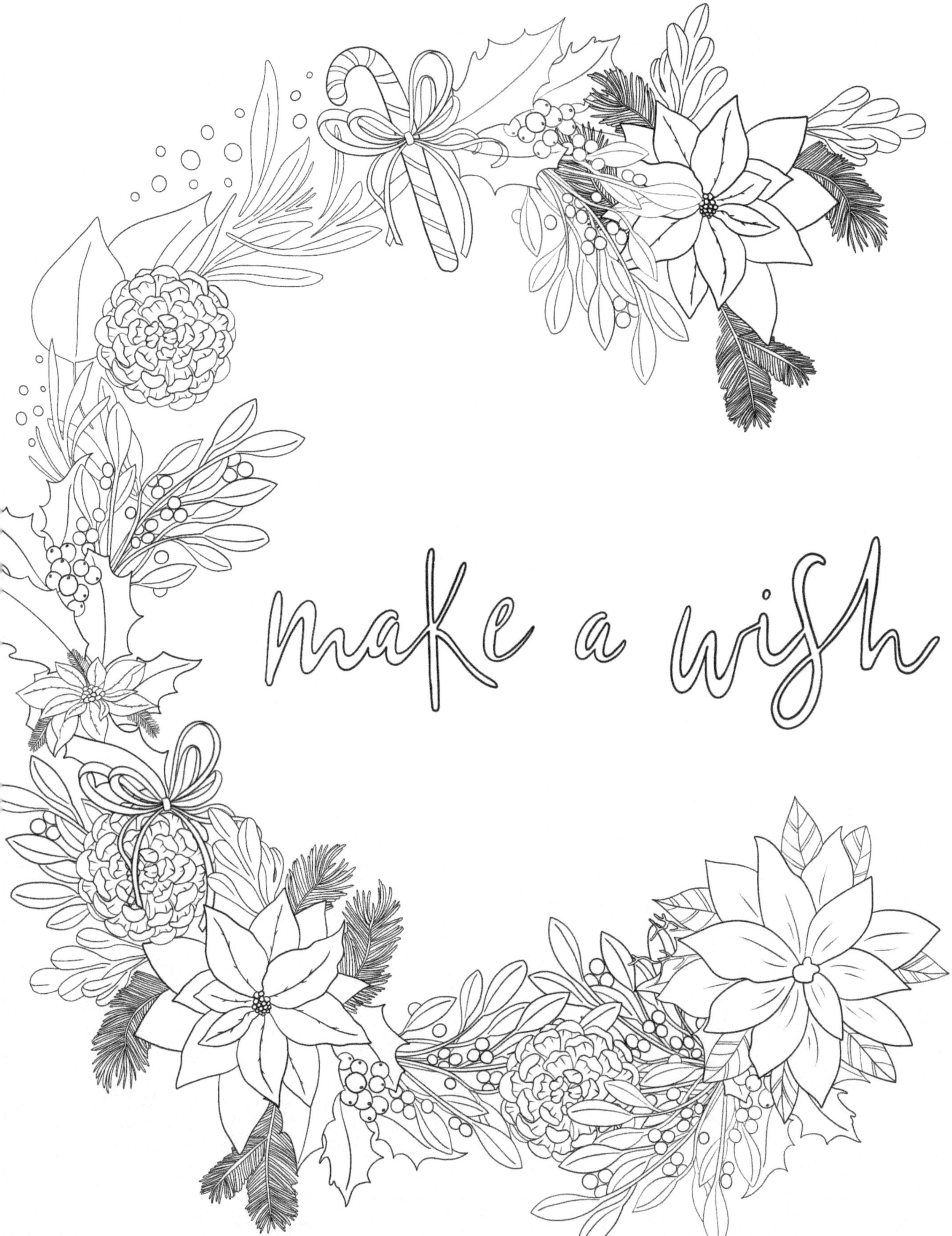
make a wish

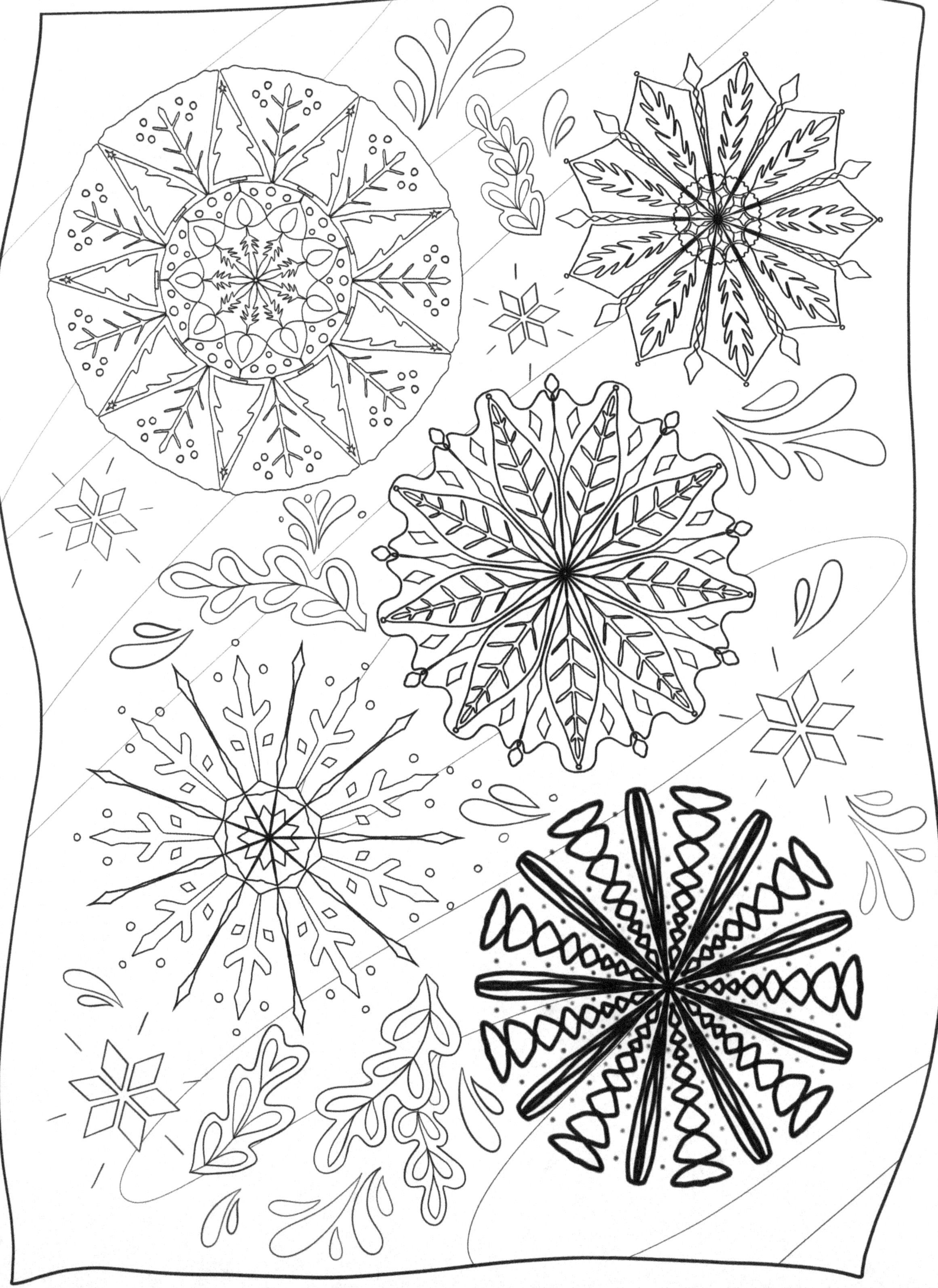

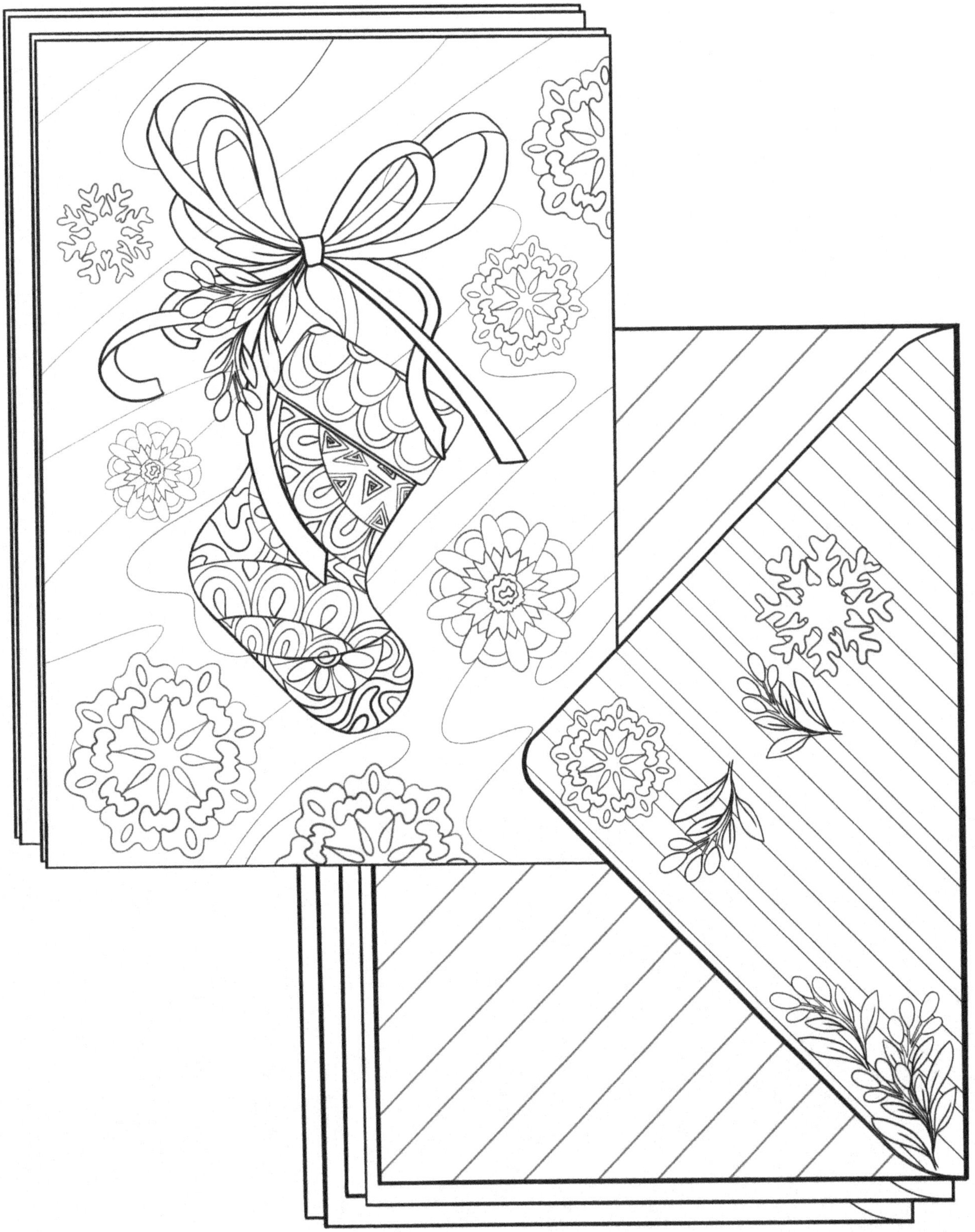

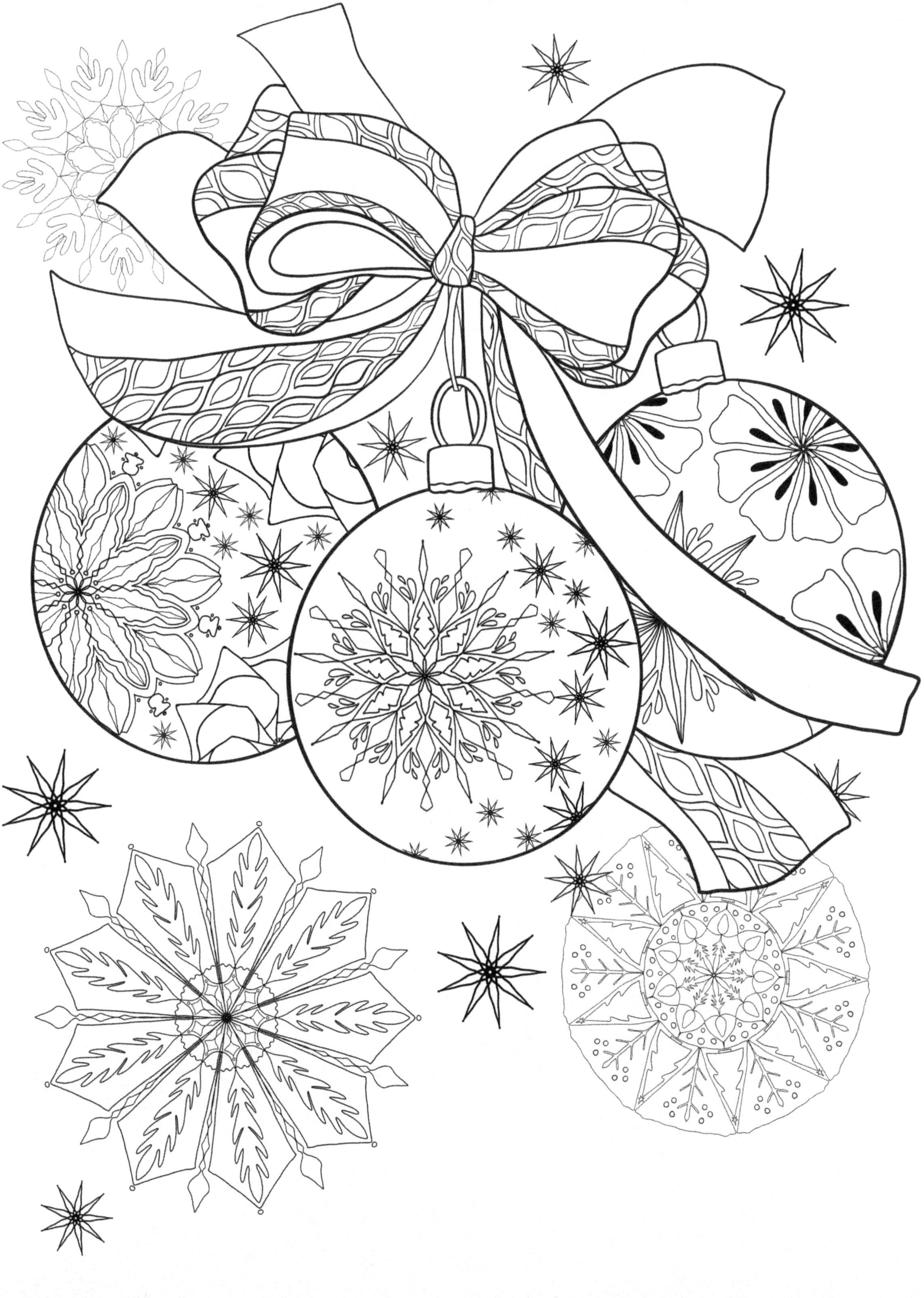

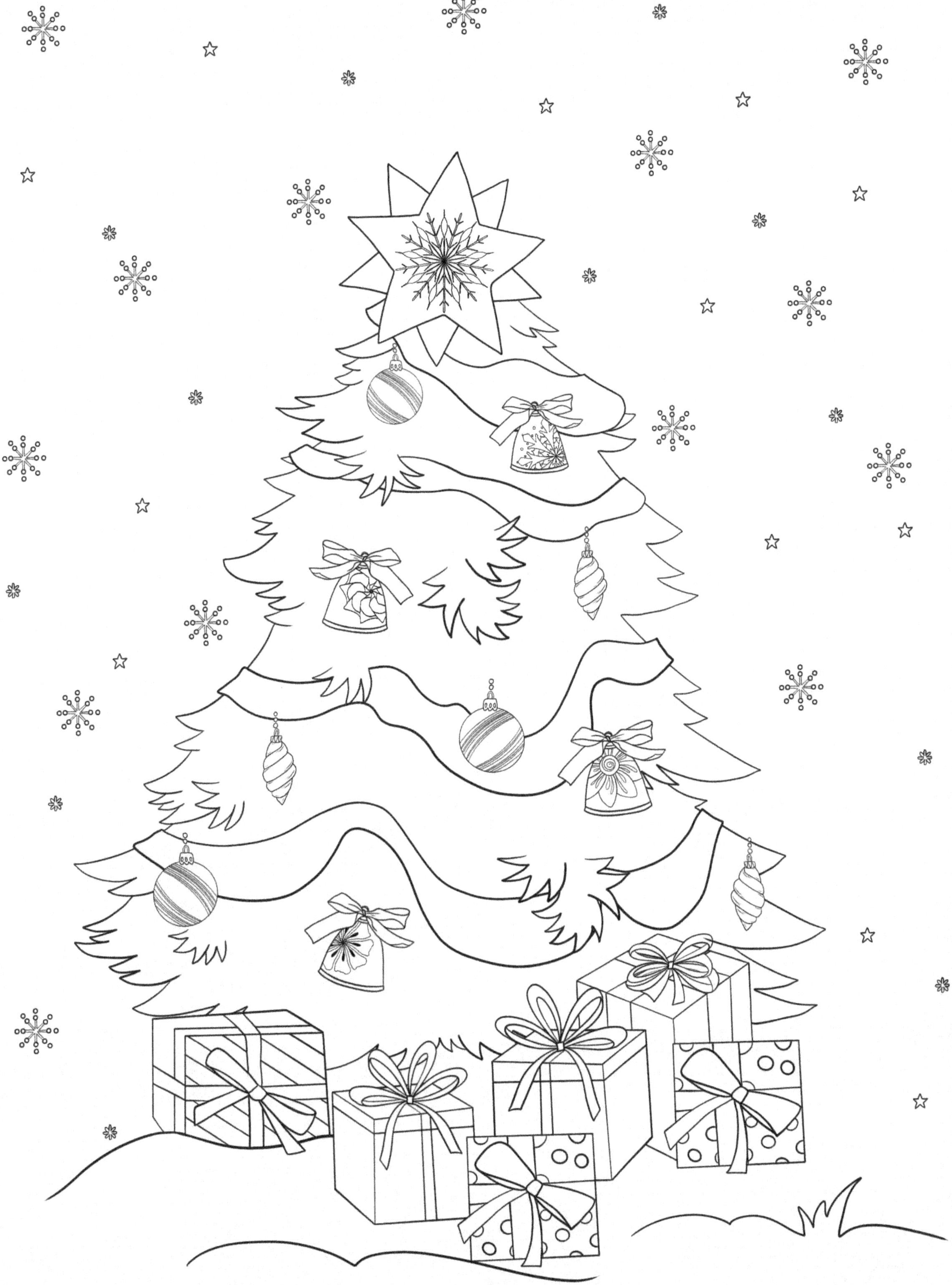

www.ingramcontent.com/pod-product-compliance
Lightning Source LLC
Chambersburg PA
CBHW080814220526
45466CB00011BB/3562
9798582630180